I0816445

KITTENS

A First Look

ANNA ANDERHAGEN

GRL Consultant, Diane Craig, Certified Literacy Specialist

Lerner Publications ◆ Minneapolis

Educator Toolbox

Reading books is a great way for kids to express what they're interested in. Before reading this title, ask the reader these questions:

> What do you think this book is about? Look at the cover for clues.
>
> What do you already know about kittens?
>
> What do you want to learn about kittens?

Let's Read Together

Encourage the reader to use the pictures to understand the text.

Point out when the reader successfully sounds out a word.

Praise the reader for recognizing sight words such as *to* and *in*.

TABLE OF CONTENTS

Kittens

Baby cats are called kittens. They are born with their eyes and ears closed.

Kittens can see and hear at about two weeks old.

When they are hungry, kittens meow to their mom.

What do you do when you are hungry?

Kittens drink their mom's milk.

Kittens have long whiskers. They help kittens feel around.

What other animals have whiskers?

When they are happy, kittens purr.

They may also move their front paws back and forth.

Kittens love to play and hunt. They chase toys.

Kittens like to jump and climb.

They love to hide in boxes.

Where do you like to hide?

Cats can live for fifteen years or more.

Some kittens love hugs!

You Connect!

Have you ever seen a kitten?

What is something you like about kittens?

How do you like to play?

STEM Snapshot

Encourage students to think and ask questions like scientists. Ask the reader:

What is something you learned about kittens?

What is something you noticed about kittens in the pictures in this book?

What is something you still don't know about kittens?

Photo Glossary

Learn More

Culliford, Amy. *Super Cute Kittens*. New York: Crabtree Publishing, 2023.

Geister-Jones, Sophie. *Cats*. Minneapolis: Pop!, 2020.

Jenner, Caryn. *Cats and Kittens*. New York: DK Publishing, 2020.

Index

Photo Acknowledgments

The images in this book are used with the permission of: © FamVeld/Shutterstock Images, pp. 4–5; © Olga Rolenko/ Shutterstock Images, pp. 6–7, 23 (top left); © Ermolaev Alexander/Shutterstock Images, p. 8; © Rashid Valitov/ Shutterstock Images, p. 9; © InterStudio/Shutterstock Images, p. 10; © McLey/Shutterstock Images, pp. 10–11, 23 (bottom right); © beton studio/Shutterstock Images, p. 12; © hitryuliya/Shutterstock Images, pp. 13, 23 (top right); © Vera Aksionava/Shutterstock Images, p. 14; © Dean Drobot/Shutterstock Images, pp. 14–15, 23 (bottom left); © Egor Klimovich/Shutterstock Images, p. 16; © newsony/Shutterstock Images, p. 17; © CEXM/Shutterstock Images, pp. 18–19; © Anna Pasichnyk/Shutterstock Images, p. 20.

Cover Photograph: © Tsekhmister/Shutterstock Images

Design Elements: © Mighty Media, Inc.

Lerner Publications Company
An imprint of Lerner Publishing Group, Inc.
241 First Avenue North
Minneapolis, MN 55401 USA

For reading levels and more information, look up this title at www.lernerbooks.com.

Main body text set in Mikado a Medium.
Typeface provided by Hannes von Doehren.

Library of Congress Cataloging-in-Publication Data

Names: Anderhagen, Anna, author.
Title: Kittens : a first look / Anna Anderhagen.
Description: Minneapolis : Lerner Publications, [2025] | Series: Read about baby animals (read for a better world) | Includes bibliographical references and index. | Audience: Ages 5–8 | Audience: Grades K–1 | Summary: “Kittens can be cuddly and fluffy, but they can also be playful and mischievous. Full-color photographs and engaging text support young readers who want to learn about baby cats”—Provided by publisher.
Identifiers: LCCN 2023033619 (print) | LCCN 2023033620 (ebook) | ISBN 9798765626382 (library binding) | ISBN 9798765629505 (paperback) | ISBN 9798765636688 (epub)
Subjects: LCSH: Kittens—Juvenile literature.
Classification: LCC SF445.7 .A53 2025 (print) | LCC SF445.7 (ebook) | DDC 636.8/07—dc23/eng/20221117

LC record available at https://lccn.loc.gov/2023033619
LC ebook record available at https://lccn.loc.gov/2023033620

Manufactured in the United States of America
1 - CG - 7/15/24